In the Catskill Mountains

A Personal Approach to Nature

In the Catskill Mountains

A Personal Approach to Nature

Walter F. Meade

Purple Mountain Press

Fleischmanns, New York

For my daughter, Donna, who encouraged me
to continue in photography, and

For my wife, Ginny, who served as editor
for this manuscript.

First Edition, 1991
Published by **PURPLE MOUNTAIN PRESS, LTD.**
Main Street, P.O. Box E-3, Fleischmanns, New York 12430

Library of Congress Cataloging-in-Publication Data

Meade, Walt.
    In the Catskill Mountains : a personal approach to nature / Walter
F. Meade. -- 1st ed.
      p.   cm.
    ISBN 0-935796-20-7 : $25.00
    1. Meade, Walt. 2. Photographers--New York (State)--Biography.
3. Nature photography.   I. Title.
TR140.M378A3 1991
770'.92--dc20
[B]   91-12887
                                                   CIP

Printed in Hong Kong
Blaze International Productions, Inc.

CONTENTS

PREFACE

This book is about the wild creatures and plants that inhabit the Catskills alongside modern-day people. More often than not they reside nearby, completely undetected — usually living with little or no help from humans. But when people do chance upon their wild neighbors, they find the discovery most rewarding.

In the following pages, I attempt to show how my life with nature developed. My introduction to the outdoors came when my family moved from the main street of the village to the countryside. Although only a small boy at the time, I soon discovered some of the neighborhood's wild creatures. A few understanding adults were helpful and encouraged me to use books to build on my experiences afield, but not everyone was supportive when I defended the right of a great-horned owl to live — in spite of its macabre ways. By this time, in my teenage years, I had become so hooked on nature that I could not condone the senseless destruction of any animal, prey or predator.

The prospect of being surrounded by nature every day of the year was a powerful inducement for me, as an adult, to choose dairy farming for my profession. Perhaps it was a greater sensitivity, engendered by my daily contact with wildlife, that led me to begin photographing birds, animals, and plants. For several years the farm routine and wildlife photography filled my days.

Slowly the dairy industry became impractical for side-hill farms, as we call steep hillside farms in the Catskills, so I closed out my operation and took a position at the Manhattan Country School Farm, teaching nature and farming to the students. Outdoor classes were especially rewarding experiences for me, because I had a chance to show the children the fascination and excitement of the natural world.

It is my hope that the words and pictures in these pages will motivate readers to discover some of the wild creatures that live in the fields and woods around their own homes, and to ensure that their wild neighbors will have a place to live in the future.

American Toad   *Bufo americanus*

CHAPTER 1

THE BUDDING NATURALIST

I was a small boy when my family moved from the main street of the village of Roxbury in the Catskill Mountains to another house far out in the countryside. At first the big, open fields and dense woods frightened me because there were no other houses close by. But there was a small brook that beckoned as it gurgled slowly along below our garden. When I saw my first frog sitting on a grassy bank beside a small pool, I began my life as a student of nature.

New discoveries cropped up almost daily as I followed the stream from pool to pool, turning over countless stones just to see what lived under them. I didn't know the names of the various insects I found crawling on the underside of the stones. But the crayfish made me laugh when I dug them out of their dens because they would scoot backwards through the water.

More exciting than all the other creatures I found in this brook were the speckled trout. At first I always scared them and they dashed under big stones to hide, leaving only a trail of muddy water behind. Soon I learned to crawl to the edge of the bank and slowly peer down into their pools without frightening them away. What a sight, to watch six or eight of these beautiful fish as they lay near the bottom. They faced into the current with their tails slowly waving back and forth like flags in the breeze. Occasionally, one of the trout would rise to the surface and snatch an insect that was floating by; then it would settle back to its position near the pool's bottom. I watched the wild trout time after time and, during these outings, I was pestered by the ever-present horde of insects: they buzzed, they crawled and they hummed wherever I walked or sat. I soon learned that most were harmless. Some, like ants, were a nuisance but the bees and hornets really hurt.

There were other astonishing insects that I encountered that summer. Little beetles that I never noticed during the day turned into the most exciting bugs of my young life when it became dark. One night they filled the air and covered the grass with countless small blinking lights. I was sure they were sparks from some big fire and ran into the house to tell my mother that we were all going to burn up. She laughed and told me the sparks were only lightning bugs.

The hired man from the farm up the road told me that dragon flies were "the devil's darning needles," and said that they could sew up small boys' ears. But when I warned my parents of this new fact, they assured me that it was just another of the unkind jokes older people played on young kids. They reminded me that a few years before, when we lived in the village, I had chased robins around the yard with a salt shaker in my hand. The milk man had told me that if I put salt on a bird's tail I could pick it up. How blessed I was to have parents who helped me to understand what I saw and who also encouraged me to keep on looking.

During my first winter in our back hollow home, father showed me some animal tracks in the snow. It was exciting for me to know that a fox or raccoon or some other animal had passed by our home during the dark of night. I learned by myself to track the cotton-tailed rabbits to their holes. One day while tracking rabbits I found a place in the snow that was littered with rabbit fur and fresh blood, but there were no tracks of the fox or bobcat that had caught it. Completely puzzled, I had to seek help from my parents. Dad showed me some wing marks in the snow that I had failed to notice and explained that I had found the works of a great-horned owl.

A red squirrel lived in a butternut tree beyond our garden. Our whole family disliked it because it always got the butternuts before they fell to the ground, where we could gather them. There were never any gray squirrels near our house, but there were chipmunks. Mother complained about them when they carried away the cracked corn she had put in the chicken feeders. I liked them because they were fairly tame. One chipmunk had a burrow near the path that we used to go to the vegetable garden, and I was able to tame this one to eat from my hand. It was my job some of the time to feed the chickens and gather the eggs. On the days I fed the chickens I always put some cracked corn in my pocket for the chipmunk — I just didn't tell anyone.

First, I offered the corn to this chippy by putting it on the ground while I sat nearby. As it got bolder in approaching the corn I moved closer until I could offer the corn from my hand and the chipmunk would take it. I was delighted to watch this little squirrel take the pieces of corn from my palm and stuff them in its cheek pouches. When its cheeks could hold no more it dashed away and vanished into its den. Within a minute or two it reappeared with empty cheeks. This behavior continued until the last piece of corn had been carried into the den. The chipmunk was always busy adding to its hoard of seeds, nuts and small fruits, which it stored in the den to live on during the long winter months when it was inactive.

During my second summer I was allowed to fish the brook for trout. I started with a pole cut near the stream, a short piece of line, and a small hook. My bait was worms dug in our garden or grasshoppers caught in the fields later in the summer. Once I began to catch trout, the stream shared an equal place in my life with the dinner table. I only stopped fishing when I became so hungry I couldn't stand it any longer.

My many hours spent along the stream gradually led to a study of trout behavior. I learned the best times of day to fish and the best places to float my bait. I would seek trout beside boulders, under sunken logs, and beneath undercut banks.

During my quest for trout I ranged further from the house and stumbled upon many more inhabitants of the streamside. Several times each day as I was fishing, woodchucks watched me from their holes and cotton-tailed rabbits dashed into the thick brush. Once in a while a muskrat would appear in the stream, but my greatest thrill occurred late one rainy afternoon when a mink bounded into view. At the sight of me it stopped and stood up. Its long weasel-like body stretched to its full height as it studied me with its beady eyes. The soft, dark brown fur along its sides glistened even in the dull light of the rainy afternoon. This incessant traveler could pause to look at me only briefly, for suddenly it turned and hopped on down along the stream's bank and out of my sight. Little did I know that later I might meet this mink or one very much like it.

My mother kept her laying hens in a large chicken house that was built near the stream, just east of the garden. One night, late in the summer, it was raided. Twenty-four chickens were killed. I remember the dead chickens covered with their own blood, lying wherever they had died. The chicken house floor was littered with feathers. Lots of feathers. Feathers filled the water dish and the feed trough. It looked like a battlefield after the armies had retreated. The chickens that were still alive acted dazed, unwilling to move.

Who had been this cruel, senseless killer? After a search we found a hole under the chicken house door and it was here that Dad thought the predator had gained entrance. A trap was set nearby. If the invader returned, we would find out what it was and put an end to its costly mischief.

I was the first one up next morning because I had to know if we had caught the chicken killer. I ran up the path along the brook that led to the chicken house. Yes, there was something in the trap, but I couldn't see it. The dirt was freshly dug up and the trap was pulled back under the chicken house. The killer was out of sight. What could it be? I turned and sprinted back to the house, yelling at the top of my voice for Dad to come because we had something in the trap.

Within minutes our whole family was gathered around, as Dad took hold of the trap chain and started to pull gently. But the hidden perpetrator resisted exposure, so much so that we had to get a stick and dig a larger hole under the hen house. Then Dad took hold of the trap chain again and pulled a large, very angry mink into view. The mink was declared guilty for two good reasons: because it had tried to enter the chicken house again and because the method of killing was typical of mink behavior. No other proofs were needed; the mink was dispatched on the spot. Dad's assessment proved correct, for the survivors of our nearly ruined flock never suffered another attack.

I was excited when we caught the raider and killed it, but I remembered the mink I saw on the stream bank, and how it had thrilled me. Any mink has to hunt and kill to live. But what made the difference between a good mink and the bad mink we had just trapped? If a mink caught a field mouse no one cared, but when the same mink destroyed our chickens it had to be killed. This was my first lesson in how differently people look at wildlife. It was all very puzzling for a young boy who knew nothing about the relationships between humans and wild creatures.

The out-of-doors had grown from my playground into my classroom during our stay at this countryside home. My greatest thrills came from encountering the birds and animals that I unexpectedly met in my wanderings. Every new adventure only increased my craving for still more wildlife meetings until such ramblings became the way of my young life. Father and I often took walks afield on Sunday afternoons and these hikes helped me develop my budding detective skills. He not only explained the tracks we found in the dust and mud, but told me many exciting stories about his own outdoor experiences. My life was being shaped by my father's words and my joyful days outdoors.

One night at the supper table my world crashed when my parents informed us children that we were all moving back to the village. I was the only one who objected and I did it loudly; but of course it was futile. Our new home was near Dad's work, and it had been purchased, not just rented. The move was a very positive step for the family and I was made to feel ashamed for my selfishness. I knew my parents were right and I was wrong. But the last time I looked back up the road as we drove away from the big fields, the woods, and the brook — I felt an uncomprehending sorrow.

Great Horned Owl   *Bubo virginianus*

CHAPTER 2

THE BOY AND THE OWL

Our new home was located on the outskirts of the village not far from some woodlands. We had not lived there long before I began exploring the forest, looking for the birds and animals I had gotten to know on the mountainside. I soon found most of my old friends but there were a great many new ones that I knew nothing about. I began reading every book on nature I could find at school and in the local library.

It was during my search for the identification of a certain hawk that I learned about great-horned owls and their unusual nesting habits. It seemed impossible to me that they could nest in late winter, ignoring both the cold and snow. How could any bird keep its eggs warm during a snow storm? All I knew about these big owls was what I had read in books. I wanted to see them for myself.

Dad assured me that we lived in a good location to find nesting owls. Although I was not aware of them, he had heard great-horned owls hooting in the woods above our house. Many nights when I went to bed I tried to stay awake as long as I could, hoping to hear them. But I always fell asleep before they began calling. One December evening during the start of a snowstorm my mother asked me to take a walk with her, for she enjoyed tramping about in the snow. We had not gone very far when a great-horned owl hooted from the hemlock forest above our house. We stopped and listened. Its loud booming voice was persistent as it questioned the night, "Who, who, who?" While we stood listening to the inquisitive owl, my mother noticed I was trembling and asked if I was cold. I said, "No, no, I am just excited. . . Some day I am going to find that owl's nest."

However, it was more than two years before I was actually able to locate an owl's nest. High in a large white pine tree, the owls were brooding in a hawk's nest, left from the previous summer. Great-horned owls commonly appropriate the nests of hawks, crows, and even grey squirrels, instead of building nests of their own. They nest so very early in the season that there is no competition for any of the unused nests. Snow and cold don't deter these big owls from starting their families when most other birds and animals are struggling just to survive the cruelest part of winter.

I had walked quite close to the big pine tree before I saw the owl on its nest. The female, larger than the absent male, was nearly covered with snow. I noticed her movement when she flattened herself down as low in the nest as she could. Her big round head, with long ear tufts and large yellow eyes, strongly resembled that of a big cat.

Every day or two after school I checked the nest. No matter how careful I was in approaching the nest, I could not get near it without being seen by the owl. Even though she knew I was there, she did not fly away, but stayed to protect her eggs. I hid in a little hemlock thicket watching for the male who must be supplying his mate with food, but he never came. I found the partly eaten bodies of three cotton-tailed rabbits, very likely dropped by the owls near the base of the nest tree.

Every time I visited the white pine tree the big female was on the nest. When I arrived one afternoon, I was shocked to find that she wasn't anywhere to be seen. I jumped to conclusions. I was sure someone had killed her. While brooding her eggs she would have been vulnerable to anyone with a gun, because when approached she would have been reluctant to leave her eggs.

I was angry. Some of the local hunters had pressured me to tell them where the nest was because they wanted to shoot the owls and destroy their eggs. Had I inadvertently given away the nest's location? It was days before I returned to the nest, for I was tormented constantly with the loss of the owls. I felt to blame for their demise.

After a few weeks, I went back to the old nest site in search of clues about the owl's disappearance. Even from a distance I realized my mistake, for I could see two half-grown owlets perched on the edge of the nest. Immediately, I was aware that I had misinterpreted the earlier absence of the female owl; she had only left the nest because the eggs had hatched and she was helping the male hunt for the youngsters' food.

I was so excited I ran the last hundred yards to the nest. Watching the owlets for several minutes, I decided to retreat to the hemlock thicket and see if one of the adults would return to the nest with food for the young. Statue-like, I remained there, moving only my eyes, and after nearly two hours' wait one of the adults came to the nest bearing a red squirrel. When

I left it was so dark I could barely see to pick my way out of the woods. All the way home I vowed over and over to myself that I would not tell anyone the owls were alive.

I returned to the owls' nest every day after I got home from school. Now as I approached the big pine tree the adult owl left her youngsters in the nest, flew a short distance away, and perched in a tree where she could watch me. I soon learned what efficient hunters the parent owls were, for the ground under the nest tree became littered with partly eaten remains of their prey. Cotton-tailed rabbits comprised most of the young owls' diet. However, there were scraps of other species such as grouse, pheasants, both red and gray squirrels, a weasel, a chipmunk, and several heads and fins of sucker fish. The little ones grew well on the generous offerings from the adults and in a few weeks the owlets filled the nest.

As I neared the nest tree late one April afternoon, I noticed a movement on the ground. I rushed over to see what it could be and found that one of the young owls had fallen out of the nest. It was much larger than it had appeared when it was high up in the nest—all of fifteen inches high. Brownish-gray down and sprouting wing and tail feathers covered its body. The owlet confronted me with a bold show of savagery: It hissed at me, clicked its beak threateningly, and glared at me with two big yellow eyes that seemed to radiate hate. Realizing that it could not fly, I walked very close to it. There was no way I could replace the young owl in the nest. I couldn't even reach down to pick it up, because it was ready to attack me with its eight needle-sharp talons if I was foolish enough to let one of my hands come within their reach.

How could I transport this vicious bird home? For lack of a better idea, I took off the heavy handknit sweater I was wearing and dropped it on the owl. Instantly, it drove all eight talons deep into the woolen strands and locked the threatening claws fast. It was determined not to let go. I simply picked up the sweater and owl and carried them home.

The capture had been a success, but I had one more big obstacle before I could hope to have a pet owl: I must convince both my parents that keeping it was a good thing to do. My father thought it wrong to raise an enemy of other wildlife. My mother was even more emphatic in her objection, stating flatly that she had enough to do without taking care of a hostile owl. There was a lot of talk back and forth, most of it not good either for me or for the owl. My older sisters failed to see any great qualities in this owl. They simply dubbed it "the savage little beast."

I built a large wire-covered pen even before I had my parents' permission. I thought it might help my cause, and I think it did, for finally both parents said, "It is your bird, Walt, and you have to take care of it." Thus began an instructive, three-year relationship between a great-horned owl and a boy.

I spent many hours with my owl, hoping it would become so used to me that it would allow me to handle it. This was only wishful thinking, for whenever I got close it was ready to fight. I tried offering it food from my hand and it worked a few times. Then I became over-confident and paid the price for my carelessness. The owl grabbed my hand instead of the food in it.

When the owl grew to adulthood, it surprised everyone by how efficiently it could catch rats. Charlie, our next-door neighbor, remarked to many people, "Walt's owl is the best rat trap I've ever seen." There were three chicken houses in the vicinity where we lived, my mother's and two others, each harboring many rats. Often they moved from one chicken house to the other, and their path went directly across the ground where I had built the owl's pen. It was not unusual to find a couple of dead rats in the owl's pen each morning, rats that had made the mistake of entering the pen in their travels during the night. The dead rats were seldom eaten, but if the owl had devoured any part of them, it was just the head.

The owl had proven itself as a hunter not only by the large number of rats it had caught, but also by killing two of Mother's chickens. From its perch it watched the foolish chickens stick their heads through the wire fence of the pen to nip off blades of grass. The unsuspecting hens never had a chance to escape. The owl dropped from its perch with deadly accuracy, grasping their heads with its feet. The long needle-sharp talons easily pierced the chickens' brains, killing them instantly. Although the chickens beat their wings against the wire fence in a wild display of death spasms, they were dead the moment the big owl hit. The owl as a chicken killer was a sore subject in our home, for Mother took much pride in her well-bred flock.

I never grew tired of the owl. In fact, I became so fascinated with it that I started a notebook of my observations. Our neighbors were not like-minded. They considered owls varmints just because they were flesh-eaters that preyed upon domestic fowl and hunters' game. They horrified me when they demanded that my father "kill the damned owl and be done with it." But he refused to go along with them because he believed I should make any decisions that affected my pet.

Great-horned owls mate in the dead of January and they become very vocal during this winter courting season. My owl happened to be a female and attracted more than just one suitor; in fact, one night four males arrived in our neighborhood. The eager males turned a quiet evening into an uproarious night—they hooted all night long. I crawled to my bedroom window to look for the wooers and soon spotted two of the males in the dim moonlight, perched on telephone poles. The other two were in nearby trees; although I could not see them, their constant hooting told me exactly where they had settled. I was excited; four great-horned owls almost in our dooryard—a great-horned owl serenade!

Not once did the thought cross my young mind that maybe others in the neighborhood did not share my love of owl concerts. There had been some hooting for the last few weeks but nothing like tonight's performance. The tempo accelerated until it sounded like a dozen owls, not just four males and a lone female. I thoroughly enjoyed the commotion, so much so that I pulled the top quilt from my bed, wrapped it around me, and stayed by the open window most of the night. Little did I realize what troubles the morrow held for me.

Not only did our next-door neighbors come to our house to complain, but even folks from several streets away insisted the owl was a public nuisance. One man who claimed to be a great friend of all wild creatures avowed to some of the neighbors that he was going to kill the pesky owl some dark night. Another woman informed my mother that a boy who could enjoy this savage, noisy owl was not quite right in the head. Even the neighborhood kids twitted me for being strange. One thing was now becoming clear — no one liked the owl but me. My parents told me I had to do something about the owl because everyone, after nearly three years of patience, was getting fed up. They pointed out that I had failed to consider other peoples' feelings because I enjoyed the owl so much. The neighbors' solution was to shoot the owl, but I argued that the owl had a right to live. Mother convinced me I was not treating the owl fairly by keeping it in the pen and that it could survive very well on its own.

It was final. There was to be no more delaying talk — the owl was to go that day. How hard it was for me to open the pen. For so long I had guarded against any kind of mishap that might let the owl escape. I felt a little sick when I hooked the gate open. The owl did not dive through the open gate as I thought it would. It shook its body, closed its eyes, and settled down on its perch. I walked back several feet from the pen and sat down to watch. The owl went to sleep. Twenty minutes later the owl had not moved, so I ran to the house to tell my mother the owl did not want to leave. This time I was ordered to go back and drive the owl outside.

I entered the pen and forced the owl off its perch. It flew past the gate, but did not offer to fly out. I actually made four attempts before I drove the owl outside. Once out of the pen it flew some thirty feet away and alighted on a fence post. It looked back over its shoulder at me for a full minute before it took off across the open fields. I watched its powerful wingbeats reduce it from my two-foot high companion to a tiny speck that dissolved in the distance. The big owl left me as it had come to me: wild, fierce, and completely untamed.

Eastern Kingbird   Tyrannus tyrannus

CHAPTER 3

OF BEES AND BEARS

During my early teenage years I met and worked with an experienced birdwatcher, who encouraged me to augment the study of birds I had begun about the time my family and I moved back to the village. She lent me the most complete books on identification and birdlore that I had ever seen, books that taught me to recognize birds in silhouette as well as by size and color, and to distinguish the eggs and nests of many different birds. Until I read these books I knew nothing about bird families. I had no idea that a robin was kin to a wood thrush or that the bossy kingbird and the gentle phoebe were both flycatchers. Under the birdwatcher's tutelage I studied the common birds until I could readily identify not only the colorful males but also the less vivid females. Any that proved very difficult my birding teacher had me sketch with pencil and color with crayons, a practice I continue today when I encounter new birds in far off places.

My birdwatching mentor took me on my first "bird hike," a field trip devoted to observing birds and then recording the new sightings on a list. She showed me her "life list" accumulated over many years of bird watching. From her birding accounts I sensed the excitement and elation of discovering a really rare bird.

I marveled at my tutor's ability to recognize birds by their songs, from the song of the common robin to the voices of more difficult warblers. Once, while I was still searching the treetops for what turned out to be a scarlet tanager, my teacher had already identified it by its call. I did not share her special knack for recognizing birdsongs, and it took me many years of careful listening to equal her proficiency.

The notes I was in the habit of keeping by now had become diary-like reports of each day's outing. Many times I felt the need for pictures to reinforce my words in this early journal. At first I sketched images on the pages, but what I really needed were photographs. My first camera was a folding one of the 120 size, with very definite limitations for taking nature photographs. One spring day I set it up beside the nest of a pair of yellow warblers. When the adults arrived to feed their youngsters I tripped the shutter from my hiding place with a long string. The resulting pictures were terrible. They were slightly out of focus and many were under- or over-exposed. But I was delighted. Photography would be a way to make a lasting record of the birds I was watching.

Although from a very early age I had heard about digging ginseng plants and hunting bee trees, by the time I was twelve I had only participated a few times in these activities. During those early outings I had always accompanied an adult who had some knowledge of these pastimes. By following along, asking many questions and watching carefully, I had learned to identify the ginseng plant and to know where it grew. Bee hunting was much harder to learn, so I started hunting ginseng first. Ginseng had an important attraction over bee trees — its roots could be sold for cash money. Anything I could contribute to the family income was welcome.

Ginseng is certainly one of the most famous herbs growing in the world. Its root has been highly valued for centuries by the Chinese for its health-producing benefits. The wild Asian plants had been virtually exhausted when, in the 1700s, ginseng was discovered growing in southern Canada and the Colonies. Tons and tons of the wild roots were dug in eastern North American hardwood forests and shipped to China. Ginseng was harvested all summer long by an army of diggers who were ruled by greed and gave no thought to the future of the root supply. The trade lasted for many years, and by the end of that period the North American supply had suffered greatly. By the time I entered the woods as a ginseng digger the heyday of the ginseng trade was past. It was still possible to make some good finds of wild roots, but I would have to hunt very hard for them.

I was taught by my father to hunt ginseng only during the autumn season, when the mature berries of the plants I dug could be planted to ensure a future crop. During the fall season, just before the leaves die down on this perennial plant, its foliage turns a bright yellow and can be seen even by the inexperienced eye. Hunting ginseng, like many other outdoor pursuits, is a labor of love today, and ginseng hunters must practice conservation in order to preserve their sport.

Hunting wild honey was much more difficult for me than finding ginseng plants. The honey is made and stored in a hollow tree by a swarm of honeybees that has escaped from a bee yard, or apiary, within a few miles of the bee tree's location. Like me, some persons enjoy hunting these elusive swarms in the fall of the year for the honey the bees have laid up during the summer.

At first I considered myself a failure because I had found only two bee trees, and both of these by accident. The first one I managed to locate when I heard the bees humming in a hollow hemlock, as I walked through the woods one day. I came upon the second one while hunting ginseng — no skill, just good luck.

Then I met George, who was a highly skilled bee hunter. He taught me the techniques of following wild bees to their hive trees and removing the honey from them. I not only learned to hunt bees, but I also made a friendship that lasted until George's death many years later.

George showed me that when honeybees gather nectar they tend to fly a straight course from the flowers to their hive. It is this characteristic that leads bee hunters to the location of the wild bee tree. When the flowers no longer produce nectar after a killing frost in the fall, bee hunters substitute a thin sugar syrup for the nectar. They lure the bees to the sugar-water bait by using some kind of an appealing scent such as oil of sweet clover or oil of anise. Once the bees find the syrup they drink all they can hold and fly back to the hive tree. The number of bees will build rapidly once a few start taking the bait to their home. It is not unusual to have two or three hundred bees forming a stream going to and from the sugar-syrup bait. It is the bee hunters' task to watch for the exact direction of the departing bees and then to follow this line to the tree.

Bee hunting is not for everyone. When bees fail to return to the bait quickly, many people lack the patience to wait until the line of bees is established. Others become frustrated when following the line because it is difficult to distinguish the correct tree in a forest filled with trees.

When the tree is found, removing the honey combs poses a risk that discourages many would-be hunters. After cutting down the tree, the hunters expose the honey hollow by sawing into the side of the tree, then use an ax to split away the last pieces of wood that cover the honey. Make no mistake; the person who removes the final wood slabs from the hollow is greeted by hundreds of very angry bees, and is sure to be stung several times. In spite of the painful stings, this is a very exciting time; the hunters may uncover a hive that is worthless or one that contains up to 40 or 50 pounds of wild honey.

After an autumn of bee hunting, the shelves of our family larder were lined with jars of honey, enough that my parents could exchange it with neighbors for garden vegetables. But wild honey was not a cash crop, and because it was less lucrative than ginseng I usually hunted bees later in the fall, only after the ginseng tops had died down and disappeared. The pastime that produced family income had priority.

It was also to help support the family that I started hunting red foxes. Because of the Great Depression, there was little or no work for adult men, let alone for a teenage kid. A raw fox fur did not bring a large sum of money, but neither did anything else. It seemed so simple, as red foxes usually spend the daylight hours sleeping somewhere above ground and I thought I could easily track one to its bedding place and shoot it. How much I had to learn before I was finally able to shoot my first fox.

My first winter season as a fox hunter I spent tracking a number of foxes, but all I ever found were their round beds in the snow and their fresh tracks as they leaped away. I failed to get a shot at even one. I needed help from someone who knew more about still-hunting foxes than I did. Old-time fox hunters that I knew all told me the same thing, "Get yourself a good hound — you will never shoot many foxes by tracking them up." But I had to learn how to hunt foxes without a dog because I didn't have the money to buy one.

At last I heard of an old man named "Rube" who had a reputation as a still-hunter of foxes. During the summer I made the 25-mile trip to his home and spent a day talking with him. Rube was very old, with a full beard and a bald head. He laughed and said, "They put my hair in the wrong place." The first few minutes I was there he looked at the floor, not at me. With his eyes half shut, he twisted the end of his beard between his thumb and first finger. Slowly he turned, looked straight at me and said, "Son, you want to talk about still-hunting foxes."

"Yes," I said, "but everyone thinks I'm foolish to try it."

"Well, you're not," Rube said. "It does have some drawbacks compared to dog-hunting, but it's a lot more sporting than hunting with a dog because you are matching your wits against the fox . . . not just standing on a runway, freezing to death while the hound does all the leg work. Nope, I have owned some good hounds, but I like to hunt foxes just by myself, best of all."

Then Rube began to tell a series of hunting stories about how he had outwitted some of the smartest foxes in the whole countryside. Suddenly I was aware that Rube was sitting on the edge of his chair — his eyes were wide open and he was looking at me, not at the floor. "You will walk a lot of miles for every fox you get," Rube warned, "but there are worse things in this world than walking. The worst I can think of is being so old you can't walk any more," he said as he pointed to his own legs.

Rube gave me a lot of good tips on how to hunt and track, how to walk quietly in the snow, and how to approach a sleeping fox. Like my mentor the birdwatcher, he advised me to keep notes of my experiences in the field. These careful records became the key to my success as a still-hunter.

I kept a detailed account of every hunt, regardless of its outcome, putting more emphasis on the foxes that outsmarted me than on the ones that I bagged. After the first winter of well-documented but futile hunts, I was able to discover many of my mistakes, and with each new season I gathered more evidence about the subtle behavior patterns of the foxes I was trying to outwit. The written record taught me the most productive hours of the day in which to hunt, and the best snow conditions in which to approach a fox. Soft, fluffy snow, for example, is best for hunting foxes; any snow that squeaks or crunches underfoot will surely alert the bedded fox.

Each year I analyzed my "foxology" notes and the information I gained resulted in bigger and bigger harvests of foxes. The very people who said that still-hunting was fool-headed now wanted to know how I did it. I was reluctant to give away my hard-earned knowledge; nevertheless, I shared some of my insights with a few close friends. They were not willing, however, to walk the miles that still-hunting required. Before the first season was over, all had quit, saying it could not be done, that I had not told them the real secret of still-hunting. I knew that still-hunting could be successful, and continued to bag foxes by this method because I was willing to walk many miles for every fox I got.

Long before reaching my teenage years I had learned that outdoor persons stumble upon the most interesting finds when they are in pursuit of something else. One day I had taken a pail and gone to the head of the hemlock woods to pick wild blackberries. This area supported some very large hemlock trees, several hemlock thickets, many deciduous trees, two big mossy swamps and a trout stream. Often I had fished there and had walked the muddy old wood roads looking for song birds. It was a good blackberry year and I was sure to find a crop in the clearings among the hemlocks.

Shortly after I started down one of the old log roads I came to a halt in mid-stride. I was about to step in a large bear's track in the mud — the first bear track I had ever seen. I studied the hind foot impression and compared it to ones I had seen in books. The pad was about eight inches long and the claw marks showed clearly. The track appeared to be at least a day old. According to the stories I had heard Dad tell about how far bears travel, the bear could be miles away by now.

I went to the first big blackberry patch and found it flattened as if a land roller had gone back and forth over the canes. Then I noticed heaps of what could only be bear droppings. The bear must have fed here several times before it had finished off all the berries. Just below the ruined berry patch was an open field where I noticed very large stones turned over, stones bigger than two men could handle. The 300-pound animal had turned over the huge stones just to lick up the tiny ants that lived beneath.

I forgot about picking berries; instead I searched for more signs of the bear. There were several other places where the bear had turned over stones, and I could see that it had broken down a number of large chokecherry bushes to get at the fruit. I left the hemlock woods late in the afternoon, tired but very excited and without a single berry in my pail.

Once home, all I could talk about were the bear signs I had found. No one even bothered to ask why I had failed to bring home any blackberries. But my oldest sister asked in a snickering way if she could put a crust over a "bear story pie" like the one on a blackberry pie. Mother ignored the remark because she was concerned for my safety. She thought it very dangerous for me to be in an area occupied by a bear. Dad calmed her fears by saying that he was sure the bear had left the swamp once I disturbed it.

A few days later I returned to the hemlock woods, not for berries, but for another look at the bear signs. Within minutes after entering the evergreen woods, I knew Dad was wrong: I found fresh bear tracks in the mud. Like a hound searching for a scent I looked everywhere for more clues to the bear's stay in the evergreen woods. I discovered many tracks and droppings along the path I was following. The wilted tops of jack-in-the-pul-pit plants lay everywhere. The bear had scooped the shallow-rooted perennials out of the ground with its claws and had bitten off the fiery tuber. The bear had not left a standing plant that I could find.

It was in the thick hemlock swamp that I found the freshest and most impressive signs of the bear. The hot, muggy, late-August day had brought out swarms of mosquitoes who were eating me alive as I followed the muddy path deeper into the swamp. I was about to turn back because of the constant irritation when I came upon a depression that had clearly been dug by the bear. This muddy, sunken bowl was about ten inches deep, three by four feet wide and contained a couple of inches of water in the bottom. Nearby I found two more bear wallows. This bear was staying cool by bedding in the mud during the hot summer day. The mosquitoes had been bothering it too, because I noticed a couple of hemlock trees eight or ten inches in diameter that the bear had been using to scratch itself. They were plastered with dried black mud and a few of the bear's body hairs.

Further along the main path that led to this wallow area I found a tree that had been bitten or clawed, and there was a maze of bear tracks in the mud around the base of the tree. The bark and some of the wood under it was ripped loose from the tree about six to seven feet above the ground. Apparently the bear was marking its territory by tearing at the tree with teeth and claws.

In spite of all these signs, I assumed that my presence in the swamp had driven the bear out and that it had retreated up the mountainside. Indeed, I had not seen or heard the bear either time I had been in the hemlock woods. I realized my mistake when, walking back along the muddy trail, I found in several places that the bear had stepped onto my tracks. The print of his hind foot clearly obliterated the mark made by my shoe earlier in the day. The bear had never left the swamp!

I looked around and suddenly became aware that I could not see 30 feet in any direction. The high cinnamon ferns, the tall grass and the numerous hemlock thickets made this swamp a perfect hiding place for the bear. Where was it lurking? It could be within a few feet of me. Would it attack? Should I start running? No, for it would be fool-hardy to try to outrun a bear. How I wished I could just fly straight up in the air to get out of the swamp. Slowly I reasoned that the bear had known where I was all the while I was in the swamp. It was keeping out of my sight, but did not want to leave the cool refuge from the summer's heat. With great caution, I walked back out the muddy trail, taking very long steps.

Later, in the early fall, a farmer shot a big bear less than a mile from the hemlock woods. Although I visited this beautiful moss-covered swamp many times in years that followed, it was never the same. Something was missing—it needed a bear.

White-tailed Deer   *Odocoileus virginianus*

CHAPTER 4

THE FARM

There was no period in my life when I became so thoroughly immersed in nature as when my wife, daughter and I moved to the farm. Our place was a side-hill farm in the northern Catskills, and was located about 2,000 feet above sea level, near the head of one of the many hollows in the region. Like the other five farms already operating in Montgomery Hollow, ours would be a dairy farm. When we made our commitment to take up farming, we all knew it would be hard work and long hours. But we liked the idea of running our own business; and working outdoors, I would have a chance to encounter the wildlife I had been told was plentiful in this valley.

The Montgomery Hollow house was an extremely well built, wooden clapboard structure raised by a generation of builders over 100 years before. It had successfully weathered all the extremes of the elements — from near-misses of lightning to the ripping winds of both hurricanes and blizzards — without as much as a sagging rafter. When we first looked at this house we were impressed by the huge elm tree that towered over its eastern end. The elm's large, graceful limbs extended far over the roof, like a protective canopy. Inside the house cracked walls of lath and plaster formed the large rooms, and wide-board floors showed years of footwear from former occupants. The cellar door bore the teeth marks of a porcupine that had tried to gain entrance many years before. There was a muddy stain over the woodhouse door where someone had removed a robin's nest. An active spider web, with a big brown spider and three trapped flies, dangled in the corner by the chimney. The house would need a thorough cleaning before we moved in, but we had expected as much. In spite of the evidence of wear and disuse, there was a convincing air of strength and reliability about this house that made us feel secure at once.

Because the barn is the most important building on a dairy farm, housing most, if not all, of the cattle and a big share of the wintertime roughage, we examined the barn prudently. It was unpainted and weather-beaten but it had a strong, straight frame and a good roof. For both the barn and the house there was a never-failing flow of gravity-fed water from springs up the hill above the building sites. The land on this farm had proved itself by producing good field crops and large cuttings of hay, year after year.

Even though I loved farming, I could never have been entirely happy as a mere cow keeper or manager of crops and grasslands. I had a passion for the untamed things, the beings lumped together under the term, "wildlife." I needed to live in an area where the deer and the hawk were as much a part of my life as the cow and the chicken. I was very happy to have found a productive farm in a valley that was known as a haven for wild creatures.

Many of my most rewarding experiences with wildlife happened during the course of my daily outdoor farm work. These serendipitous episodes often were very brief and completely unexpected, but they left a lasting impression on me. Once during a late spring season I was repairing a fence line. As I worked slowly along, tightening the barbed wires, I flushed two very young white-tailed fawns from a large clump of tall grass. Both had remained hidden during my approach, but when I almost stepped on them they jumped from cover. They leaped away some 50 or 60 feet on very young, rather unsteady legs before they stopped, turned around, and faced me. Then came the astonishing part. The larger of the two bleated softly and leapt right back to me. Both fawns returned, sniffing and bunting gently against my legs. After a few minutes they lost interest in me and with a playful kicking up of their heels, they departed. I stood for a few minutes in disbelief, thoroughly intoxicated by their playful innocence.

I was partial to the early morning hours, especially during my daily hike when I brought in the cows for the morning milking. The first light of day, when every bush talked to me with birdsong, was an excellent time to see all kinds of wild animals. Also at this hour some of the nighttime creatures were still active. Occasionally, an owl would hoot a few times before the increasing light drove it into the thicket for the day. A night-rambling raccoon, tardy in its departure to its den, might still be fishing at the cow pasture stream. And from time to time a red fox might trot boldly across the fields carrying a young rabbit to its den.

Some of my most memorable sightings have been, however, not the behindtime night prowlers, but early daylight animals and birds when they started to move about. Woodchucks seem to prefer the cool of early morning as the time to feed. Then they retire to their underground dens during the

41

heat of mid-day. Squirrels dash about soon after dawn, scolding and barking at anything that moves in the forest. Hawks glide over the fields looking for prey even before the rising sun tops the distant mountain peaks. Deer frolic in the dew-laden fields of early morning as they move towards their mid-day bedding places. So often I recall the remark of an old hunter who said, "More happens in the first hour after daylight than in any three hours of mid-day."

This was certainly true of my first encounter with a coyote. The carcass of a woodchuck shot near the garden was missing the next day and tracks of what I thought to be a medium-sized dog showed in the loose soil. Two days later, I found the remains of another woodchuck that had been eaten. Several times that week I discovered in the cow paths the same dog-shaped tracks, larger than the print of a red fox. I started to comb our entire farm for clues and found several scats, too large for a fox, that contained woodchuck hair.

The puzzle was solved a few days later on my early morning trip to fetch the cows in for milking. As I walked to the pasture gate I was stopped short by the sight of what I thought at first glance to be a huge gray fox. Other than in pictures, I had never seen a coyote but I instantly recognized it. In our mutual surprise the coyote and I stood and stared at each other for a moment.

It was a warm, muggy morning. While the coyote studied me it started to pant and its tongue lolled out, indicating it had been running hard before it saw me. It had a grayish-brown body, pointed muzzle, and large erect reddish-colored ears. It resembled a small, slender, long-legged German shepherd except that it had a wild alertness, confidence, and beauty unknown to the domestic dog. All too soon for me, it turned and loped effortlessly across the hillside and out of my sight. I cannot describe my emotions. I was overwhelmed by this incredible happening. The written account in my journal took up three full pages on August 4th, 1953. If any one else had seen coyotes in the area before this date, I was not aware of it.

How my daily contact with wildlife on the farm sharpened my senses. Unconsciously, my eyes always seemed to be searching for wild things wherever I went, and my ears were tuned for untamed sounds. I constantly read the messages written in the mud and snow, and I recorded my experiences. My outdoor journals became as much a part of my bookkeeping as the farm ledgers. When I started to photograph wildlife, I found myself searching for any kind of natural subject, whether it was a plant, an insect, a bird, or an animal. Occasionally I suffered periods of frustration because the farm work conflicted with good photographic opportunities, and it was agreed in our family that the farm work should always come first. When I did have a chance to take photographs, the successful ones were so gratifying that they far outweighed any of the disappointments.

These early photographic pursuits taught me that two things were essential if I hoped to be successful in photographing wildlife: a very good knowledge of my wild subjects and patience, lots of patience. Wild creatures are shy and retiring and, unfortunately for the photographer, never willing to pose for the camera. I had to learn to photograph animals when they were behaving naturally in their wild surroundings. When I learned to use a blind (a natural or man-made hiding place), I was able to record wild creatures moving about in their normal way, totally unaware of my presence. The blind gave me first-hand insights into my subjects' lives that I would never have experienced any other way. Using a blind is undoubtedly the best way to photograph birds in their nests or animals at their dens. I have even called gobble turkeys to my blind during their spring breeding season and photographed them while they strutted around a plastic hen decoy.

While waiting to photograph some action at a nest or a den, I have made some surprising discoveries from my hideout. One morning when I had my blind set up near a black-throated blue warbler's nest in the upper edge of our sapbush (stand of sugar maples), I was unexpectedly visited by a bobcat on its travels. The cat appeared on a stone wall some distance beyond the low bush the warblers were nesting in, much too far away for the short telephoto lens I was using. The bobcat stood statue-like on the wall for a few minutes and studied the woods below its position, then it jumped down and came straight towards my blind. My heart was truly pounding as I prepared for it to come close enough for me to take its picture. I had no difficulty locating the cat through my peep-hole in the side of the blind and thus was able to follow its every move.

The bobcat's image was still too small for a picture when it stopped, sat down, and scratched its ear with its hind foot exactly as common house cats do. Then it licked its right front paw, and yawned a big, open mouth stretch, showing me all its very sharp, intimidating teeth. I was praying under my breath, "Please come closer," when it stood up, turned and trotted back the way it had come. My last impression of this beautiful cat was its rapidly twitching tail as it disappeared over the stone wall. Even though I was disappointed, I felt very privileged because few people ever get such an intimate look into the life of the elusive bobcat.

Given the amount of time I was able to spend afield, sooner or later I was bound to meet a bear. This encounter happened on a very hot, dry August afternoon when I was making my way slowly up the mountain with a bucket of salt for the dry cows we had pastured there. It had not rained for several days and the grass was dry and brittle underfoot. The cicadas were buzzing from the treetops and a swarm of grasshoppers took wing wherever I walked. I stopped for a short breather beside a large rock surrounded by a thick growth of raspberry bushes. Soon after I stopped to rest, the dense canes began swaying violently from the actions of some intruder. In hopes of flushing out the mysterious one, I picked up a large stone and threw it close to the disturbance. Much to my surprise, out burst a cub bear! I took off chasing the cub in hopes of catching it. To this day I don't know what I would have done with a bear cub if I had caught it. Suddenly, I discovered two other cubs running alongside of me. The chase was short-lived; I was no match for the cub trio, in either speed or maneuverability. But I did stay close enough to make all three cubs scurry up an ash tree.

What a picture! Three frolicsome little cubs stared down at me, dying with curiosity. I just had to get their picture. But how? How could I keep them up the tree while I went home for my camera? Maybe if I tied my shirt around the tree trunk the cubs would not come down over it. It seemed like my only hope, so off came my shirt and I wrapped it around the trunk about five or six feet above the ground. I turned and left the tree on a run — the quicker I could get home and back the better my chances of keeping the cubs treed. When I reached the road I took one look back to make sure the cubs were still up the tree. What I saw stopped me in my tracks. The mother bear stood with her forepaws against the tree; she had already called two of the cubs down to the ground beside her and the third one was on its way. My shirt was nowhere in sight.

Our life on the farm was very satisfying to my family and me, and perhaps that is why we did not fully recognize many of the changes starting to occur in the hollow. Within a year after we moved to our place, the neighbor up the road decided he was too old to farm any longer, so he sold out and moved to the village. His leaving was only the first of many departures within the next three or four years, as several of our neighbors, for one reason or another, left their farms. After those few years only two active farms remained in the hollow. No one else succeeded the departing families; the land was left idle. Dairy farming was definitely on the decline.

How quickly nature seized the opportunity to begin reclaiming the tidy fields of several generations of farmers. Weeds and briers were the first invaders and they easily overwhelmed the farmers' clovers, trefoils and timothy. But these first attackers only prepared the way for the brush and trees that grew rapidly. The aspens, soft maples and white birches were the forerunners of the forest which evolved later. Slowly many of the fields returned to woodlands, and human farming efforts were all but forgotten. Only the stone walls remained, to this day, as the farmers' indelible signature in many hollows of the northern Catskills' hill country.

As the trees pushed their way from the mountain tops down into the valleys, some kinds of wildlife found the new landscape much to their liking. Deer thrived on the ever-increasing brush, the abandoned orchards, and the crops of remaining farmers. Beavers and wild turkeys were successfully restored to the mountain lands. Beaver ponds became common in locations were aspen trees grew beside small streams. And wild turkeys ushered in the camouflaged hunters who tried to befool the sharp eyes of the turkey with their deceptive suits. When the uninvited coyote trickled into the Catskill Mountains it became the howling songster of the dim-light hours. Slowly but surely our hollow, like many others in the Catskills, was getting wilder than in the days of the farmers' groomed fields.

These wilder days were, of course, the result of the declining dairy industry. Farming abated for several reasons: a constantly growing farm labor shortage, a changing milk market (from cans to bulk tanks), and longer hours with even less return for the operator. In the absence of once-plentiful hand labor, farmers were forced to use more and bigger machinery for which the side-hill farms were unsuited. This was my own dilemma. My wife had passed away. My daughter and other help that had assisted me for years were now grown and seeking more profitable careers of their own off the farm. In the age of machinery, our farm was not a feasible operation. After much deliberation, I decided to sell both the cows and tools, and to keep the land. With the cows gone, the wilder land would keep me in touch with the deer and the hawk, no matter what employment I found.

Ruffed Grouse   *Bonasa umbellus*

Hen Turkey   *Meleagris gallopavo silvestris*

Black-capped Chickadee   *Parus atricapillus*

CHAPTER 5

NEW CAREERS

For many years the needs of the cows dictated how I used my time each day. Although I always enjoyed farming, it was very time consuming. Now that the cows were gone, I was able to tramp the woodlands, day after day, from early morning until the twilight hours without interruption. I wanted to retrace my footsteps in places of my childhood, and to witness the changes the many years had made. I felt compelled to follow old trails, drink from my favorite springs, watch the setting sun dress up every object around me with its golden tint — and then walk slowly home in the darkness, as if I had to be out there, in the night, so that the owl could hoot or the fox could bark.

This new-found freedom brought more than just a desire to wander. I had assigned myself to photograph wildlife that I found on my rambles. The straps on my backpack tugged at my shoulders from the weight of the photographic equipment. I carried two cameras, several lenses and a heavy tripod, plus a few filters and several rolls of film, most of it color. These prepared me for any subject, whether it was mere inches away or approaching infinity. My indispensable note book and a lunch composed the only non-photographic articles in the load I would tote until nightfall each outing day.

By the time I was ready to begin my self-appointed photographic task, it was autumn. Everywhere there were brilliantly colored subjects just waiting to be recorded on film: fall flowers, colored leaves, and some striking scenery. But unfulfilled was my long-held desire to photograph creatures that wear fur or feathers. I wanted to experience the thrill of being so well-disguised that wary, wild subjects would go about their normal ways while I photographed them.

As the fall season gave way to the coming winter, I found I had been successful in recording some of the truly shy creatures. I had photographed a great-horned owl while it dozed, perched on a dead hemlock stub. Three raccoons had posed for my long lens before they were aware of my presence. And while white-tailed deer studied my grass-covered figure and stamped their front feet impatiently, I had exposed frame after frame. My photographic procedure required more than knowledge of the subjects, it also took unlimited patience and dogged perserverance. Now that I was free of farm responsibilities, I could spend hours in a blind watching a nest of great blue herons, or return day after day to observe the beavers' progress building their dam. My photographic vacation lasted about a year; it resulted in hundreds of color slides of wildlife and created a determination on my part to make nature photography the focus of the second half of my life.

As my photos became recognized by many people in the community, the number of invitations to show my slides and to lead nature walks increased. I was encouraged to write captions to accompany appealing pictures and offer them for publication. These submissions caught on, although slowly at first, and later resulted in many articles for magazines, newspapers, and newsletters — especially periodicals in which nature aware-ness and appreciation were important aims.

I was asked to speak to a group of students at the Manhattan Country School Farm about Catskill Mountain farming methods. During the ques-tion period afterwards, the students asked more about the outdoors and the exciting experiences I had had with wildlife than they did about farming. The childrens' questions showed not only how little they knew about wildlife in the area, but also how eager they were to learn about local creatures. The question and answer period far outlasted the time allotted to it. A year later, because of my interest in the students, and my background in both farming and nature, I joined the staff of the Manhattan Country School Farm.

The Manhattan Country School Farm, a branch of a racially-integrated private school, is located in the northern Catskill Mountains, about 150 miles upstate from New York City. Formerly the property was a large dairy farm, with a big farmhouse, barn and outbuildings, and fields suitable for both hay production and grazing. Uphill from the fields a large sapbush furnishes woodlands for both maple-syrup making and nature walks. A brook purls through one of the pastures near the west side of the farm — a brook of cool, clear water.

Each week during the regular school year students from the parent school in Manhattan are transported to the Catskill Mountain farm where they participate in an exceptional program for elementary school children. A class of about twenty students with two teachers arrive at the farm on Monday and depart the following Friday. At the farm the visiting children study farming, home cooking, textiles, nature and folk music. Much of the teaching in these various fields is by the hands-on method, under the guidance of staff members who are experts in their chosen fields.

When I joined the staff, I saw the school farm as a huge outdoor classroom where I could teach children to feed and care for livestock, do farm jobs, and participate in gardening and maple-syrup making. But my greatest pleasure was teaching nature studies — to kindle students' interest in natural surroundings that would last a lifetime. Much of the magnetism of nature studies results from personal discovery in the outdoors, and day after day our field trips provided unlimited opportunities.

One dry autumn, when the water level in the brook was very low, some eager students and I watched the spawning behavior of several nests of brook trout. We observed hard-working females dig their nests by thrusting their bodies vigorously into the gravel of the streambed, stirring up the small stones and letting the current of the brook move the pebbles down stream. Over and over the tireless females repeated their forceful attacks on the gravel stones until each fish had completed a depression in the stream's bottom. Here in a finished "redd," or nest, each one would lay her eggs. Nothing entertained the children more than the behavior of the jealous males. Each female's nest was guarded by a dominant male who drove away all the lesser males that might attempt to fertilize the eggs. This way only the very best of the species would reproduce.

Besides studying brook trout, each fall the students and I made several trips to local beaver ponds to watch the beavers prepare for winter. They repaired their house and their dams with sticks and then plastered over them with fresh mud. The children were amazed to find how many trees had been cut by the beavers. Lying in all directions were the trunks of trees with their limbs trimmed off. The students followed the marks dug in the leaf-covered ground where the beavers had dragged the limbs to the pond's edge. Why did the beavers haul the big branches into the water? Several children noticed the tips of the limbs sticking out of the pond near the beaver house. I explained that this was the winter food cache for the beavers to eat when the thick covering of ice on the pond would trap them in their house.

I liked the winter as a nature study period for several reasons. Birds were very easily seen in the naked woodlands and the number of species that remained as winter residents were so few that the students soon learned to identify them. Sometimes I think the chickadees were attracted by the loud voices of the children who were elated when these curious little balls of feathers alighted in the bushes only a few feet away, calling "Chickadee-dee-dee," over and over. As one older student remarked, "They never make us feel like intruders — especially when they land on our heads!"

Owls are heard far more often than they are seen. I encouraged the students to look for signs of these nighttime predators. Sometimes my classes found grim testimonies of the owls' deadly ways marked in the snow. The tell-tale tracks of some hapless mouse or rabbit suddenly came to an end, indicated only by a few drops of blood or bits of fur where the owl had seized it with its killing talons. We profited greatly when we found owl pellets in our quest for first-hand information about these mystic creatures. Owl pellets are balls of undigested fur and bones that all owls regurgitate from their last meal before feeding again. When the class examined these remains they discovered which animals made up the owl's diet. Most of the bones were from mice, shrews, voles and pieces of rabbits' skeletons, but once we found the entire skull of a ruffed grouse.

Ordinarily a group of several students on a field trip made enough noise to scare away most of the animals they had hoped to study. As a result, the students were forced to be content with seeing the signs an animal had left, rather than the animal itself. Yet with good tracking snow and a little luck, some of my classes were able to reduce the disappointing odds by stalking stealthily along the animal's trail until the creature was found and flushed out.

The follow-and-surprise method often worked with ruffed grouse who withdraw from a person's approach by running over the snow and hiding in a place that favors an escape flight. These game birds are notorious for their sudden, explosive take-offs, after allowing the hunter to come very close to them. The unexpected outburst of thunderous wings almost underfoot so unnerves the hunter that he either fails to fire his gun or misses completely if he does.

On field trips during deep snows and very cold temperatures, the ruffed grouse demonstrated an even more nerve-shattering characteristic to my students. These birds use the wonderful insulating qualities of snow to survive the coldest periods of winter. The grouse actually flies forcibly into a soft snowbank, burying itself completely. The diving bird leaves only a five-

or six-inch hole in the surface to mark its entry, but may build tunnels as much as six to ten feet long under the snow. What a surprise awaited the unsuspecting students who found the hole and were looking around for clues about its maker. The grouse became alarmed as the students' crushing footsteps came closer and closer to its hiding place under the snow. Suddenly it burst forth with a roar of wings and a shower of snow — almost in the faces of the startled intruders who were so surprised that they fell backwards in the snow.

Another animal that provided many tracking experiences for the Farm children was the snowshoe hare. A single hare can make a labyrinth of tracks in one night — a challenging test of the students' tracking skills. The children followed the tracks, hoping to find the hare at the end of the maze of footprints. The white hare, so flawlessly camouflaged in the snow-covered woods, sat tight, not moving until the student trackers almost stepped on it. Then it sprang from its bed (called a "form"), and bounded away with ten-foot leaps disappearing among the trees. We would have to follow its trail another day.

One of the older boys summed up our tracking lessons when he said, "I used to think they were just marks in the snow. Now I know they are animal tracks. . .and I can read them. I can tell a red fox from a grey fox, or a deer from a sheep. And I can tell what they are doing."

Come spring, the School Farm was busy making maple syrup. Our tracking lessons, although limited, continued even while we worked in the sapbush. The wintertime sleepy-heads were awake by the time maple sap was running, and raccoons, woodchucks, skunks and chipmunks revealed their whereabouts on the remaining snow by numerous tracks and muddy den entrances. The sap season is the period when winter fights to keep its frozen grip on the land and spring still lacks the warmth to totally break winter's icy hold. On days when spring took control and the sap was running, we worked in the sapbush; but when winter briefly regained authority, we returned to studying tracks.

Carrying buckets of sap and boiling it into syrup are the main tasks of sapping time. But maple syrupping itself has some worthwhile nature lessons. Before tapping begins, the children must identify the trees in the sapbush correctly. Almost all of them are sugar maples, but among them grow some non-sap trees: beech, basswood, soft maple, hop hornbeam, and butternut. I always took time to teach each child how to know the sugar maple by its bark texture and color, its twigs and its typical shape. Once when a fifth grader was preparing to bore the tap hole in a tree, I asked him how he knew it was a sugar maple. But instead of listing the indentification clues I had taught him, he said, "I can tell it's a sugar maple because it has a tap hole in it from last year."

At syrup-making time some birds returned from the southland, and the first plants pushed up from the leaf litter even before the fitful days of early spring were over. But as last winter's cold lost its strength and the warm sun transformed the bud into leaf, we would return from the sapbush to a full-time nature program. We studied everything we could find, often using binoculars for distant subjects and hand-lenses for ones too small to be visible to the naked eye. Now when I took students to the beaver pond, we found a variety of ferns, golden ragwort, and swamp buttercups growing over the boggy approaches to the beavers' domain. Sometimes we were lucky and heard the whimperings of young beavers from inside the big mud house as they nestled with the female. Red-winged blackbirds hovered close overhead, scolding our group constantly; mallard ducks took wing as we neared the pond, and yellow warblers chased flying insects right beside us. There was life wherever we looked.

During the last few days of the Farm's school year I introduced the youngest students to the outdoors. This was an exceptionally exciting time for me each June because something magical happens when youngsters peer into their first bird's nest, or smell their first violets, or are shown their first fawn. These original encounters with wild things create such vivid impressions that children are inspired, as I was in my childhood, to seek more insights into nature. For me, as an adult, helping children to be aware of the fascinating discoveries that await them in the outdoors was indeed a privilege.

Red Squirrel   *Tamiasciurus hudsonicus*

CHAPTER 6

AFTERWORD

Here in the northern Catskills it was the dairy cow that reigned over the countryside. Even the hillsides were patterned according to her needs. The best, the flattest land, became meadows for her winter-time food demands. And the steeper, untillable areas became pastures for her summer-time grazing. The dairy cow helped determine the abundance of some of the wildlife that would live in her sphere of influence. The woodchuck with its appetite for grass multiplied until it became a nuisance to the farmers. The red fox fared well on the wild mice and rabbits that flourished in the open fields, and for generations farmers worked the land for the cow and hunted the red fox for its pelt.

Years later, when I was a boy, the cow was beginning to lose its control of the landscape. Some of the less-fertile farms were being abandoned. And nature with its tiny weapon, the seed, started taking back those neglected acres. Brush and weeds soon smothered the stunted grass on the inferior fields as slowly a new and wilder environment was taking shape. The white-tailed deer achieved a phenomenal return to the Catskills as the cow, year after year, relinquished more and more acres to the thickets and woods, and agriculture began to decline. Beavers and wild turkeys flourished and found fitting habitats in the changing landscape. Nevertheless, the Catskills have not become a huge wildlife refuge. Instead, country homes have replaced the cow as a threat to wildlife.

This huge and sweeping change from farming to housing development is altering the character of the Catskills. Will it destory the existing habitat for wildlife? When people develop an intimate, lifelong relationship with their wild neighbors, they are less likely to allow or promote habitat destruction, and will make sure that land-use planning considers both human and wildlife needs. Without this relationship, the Catskill Mountains in the future could look like an overwhelming suburb, with no place left for the deer and the hawk.

Eastern Cotton-tailed Rabbits   *Sylvilagus floridanus*

A Personal Approach to Nature

WOOD SORREL   *Oxalis montana*

    This low, creeping plant is usually found in cool, moist woodlands here in the Catskills. In this species the five white petals are strongly veined with pink.

EASTERN BOX TURTLE   *Terrapene carolina*

Box turtles are a land species, occasionally found in or near water, though they are well-adapted for life on land.

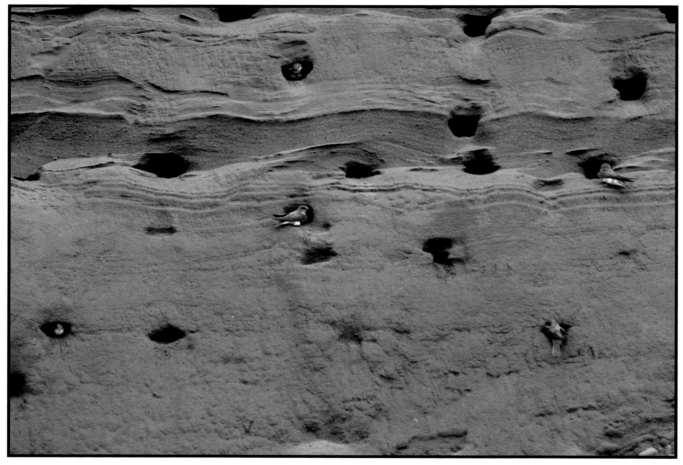

BANK SWALLOWS   *Riparia riparia*

    Bank swallows nest in steep banks that are found in sand or gravel pits and along rivers with sharp slopes. Here they build their nests by burrowing in the banks. They often form large colonies.

TWO LITTLE COONS   *Procyon lotor*

    Young raccoons are true charmers. They look so innocent and appealing that some people want them for pets. DON'T. Sooner or later most pet raccoons prove to be unsatisfactory. Besides, it is illegal to own a wild raccoon.

AMERICAN TOAD　　　　　　　　　　　　　　　　　　　　　　*Bufo americanus*

　　　　Toads choose cool, moist places to live. They are often found in cellars, under porches, and in other dark and damp hiding places.

LUNA MOTH   *Actias luna*

     This pale green moth is one of the finest big silk moths found in the Catskills. A dark, humid night during early summer is the best time to find the luna.

SPARROW HAWK   *Falco sparverius*

The sparrow hawk, or American kestrel, is the smallest and the most common falcon in the Catskills today. It hunts from poles, trees, or other high perches. It frequently hovers as it searches for its prey of mice, small snakes, or insects.

BLUE FLAG   *Iris versicolor*

This graceful, blue beauty of the marshes, wet meadows, and stream banks is similar to some of the garden iris. This wild flag with its down-curved violet sepals, that are so boldly veined, is one of the Catskills' most striking summer flowers.

ROUND-LOBED HEPATICA   *Hepatica americana*

Hepaticas, called "Mayflowers" in the Catskills, are among the very first wildflowers to bloom in the spring. The sepals of this small woodland plant vary from white and pink to violet and even deep lavendar-blue in color.

SKUNK CABBAGE   *Symplocarpus foetidus*

The impatient skunk cabbage rises up from the mud in the swamps even before winter has left the Catskills. This plant generates internal heat — warmth enough to melt its way up through ice and snow.

PAINTED TRILLIUM
Trillium undulatum

Many people feel this is the finest trillium of them all. It is certainly striking with its decorative crimson blaze in the center of its single blossom.

GREAT BLUE HERON
Ardea herodias

The great blue heron is the largest of the dark-colored herons. It is usually seen alone, standing or walking slowly in the shallow waters of the Catskills. But when nesting time arrives it becomes gregarious, and often several birds build their nests in the same tree.

FALL ASTERS   *Aster* genus

    It is the various fall asters that spread the color of royal purple over the autumn landscape. Wild asters grow in masses, but often a few blossoms make the most memorable impression.

SPAWNING BROOK TROUT   *Salvelinus fontinalis*

    Brook trout spawn during fall. The female builds a nest in the gravel where she lays her eggs. She takes a position at the bottom of the nest when she deposits the eggs, then the male darts alongside her and fertilizes the eggs as they are laid.

DEER MOUSE *Peromyscus maniculatus*

Deer mice are usually found in open habitats such as pastures, meadows, and along fence rows. But in rural areas they may also be house pests, occasionally building their nests in cupboard drawers or other secluded places.

OPOSSUM   *Didelphis virginiana*

    The opossum is the only marsupial on this continent. The female carries her young in a pouch on her belly for most of their early development. Although the opossum is considered a southern animal, it has moved northward into the Catskills within the last century.

PORCUPINE

Erethizon dorsatum

The porcupine's most striking feature is its quills. These thousands of sharp little spears give porcupines an effective defense against their enemies.

LEVERET (YOUNG SNOWSHOE HARE)   *Lepus americanus*

    The snowshoe hare is born fully-furred, eyes open, and able to crawl, unlike the rabbit that is born naked, blind, and helpless. An uncanny ability to hide is the very young hare's key to survival.

COLTSFOOT   *Tussilago farfara*

    Coltsfoot's beautiful yellow flowers burst forth from the winter-dead earth after only a few days of warm spring sunshine. The leaves do not emerge until after it blooms and seeds.

RED FOX　　　　　　　　　　　　　　　　　　　　　　　　　　　　　　　　　　　　　*Vulpes vulpes*

　　The sly red fox is renowned for its cunning and intelligence. Even when fairly common, red foxes are difficult to observe for they are shy and mostly nocturnal in their movements.

JEWELWEED
Impatiens capensis

"Jewel" is the best description for this plant's blossom — pendent jewels of red, yellow, and gold. Jewelweed has a surprise for the novice because its ripe seedpods will explode at the touch. Thus its other common name — "touch-me-not."

BARRED OWL
Strix varia

The barred owl seeks the deep, dark woods for its home. And in the middle of the night it will ask you the same question over and over, "Who cooks for you? Who cooks for you all?"

WHITE-TAIL DOE   *Odocoileus virginianus*

    The white-tail doe is wearing her red or summer coat of hair. The much-loved white-tail deer gets its name from the white underside of its tail. When it becomes alarmed it elevates the tail like a white flag and runs off.

BLACK BEAR   *Ursus americanus*

Black bears are the largest animals in the Catskills, occasionally exceeding more than 500 pounds at maturity, but they weigh only ounces at birth. Bears are always hungry and will eat almost anything they happen to find, from small insects and berries to the carrion of a deer.

BEE BALM (OSWEGO TEA)   *Monarda didyma*

The flowers of bee balm, or Oswego tea, are as intense a scarlet as can be found anywhere in nature. The fresh or dried leaves, steeped in hot water, make a desirable tea.

OX-EYE DAISY   *Chrysanthemum leucanthemum*

  The common field daisy, although beautiful, is too common for its own good. If it were as rare as the moccasin flower it would be appreciated, even treasured, but because it is so abundant few people give it a second glance.

MARSH MARIGOLD *Caltha palustris*

    As the name implies, this plant grows in swamps and wet, open woods. It is also known as "cowslip" and is a member of the buttercup family. The shiny, bright yellow, buttercup-like flowers are very conspicuous in the dead-brown swamps of early spring.

BLACK-EYED SUSAN   *Rudbeckia hirta*

  This intense yellow beauty of late summer asks little from the soil where it grows. The black-eyed susan thrives on waste land, in abandoned fields, and along roadsides where fertility is at a minimum.

GRAY FOX *Unrocyon cinereoargenteus*

This is the only fox that can climb a tree. Gray foxes, unlike their red cousins, prefer woodlands, or brushy, rocky terrain and swamps rather than open fields and small, patchy woods.

POLYPHEMUS MOTH   Antheraea polyphemus

The polyphemus silk moth lives only a short time after coming out of its cocoon. Hours later it mates and lays its eggs, then it dies. In a few days the eggs hatch into tiny larvae that feed on a number of common trees and shrubs.

WILD GERANIUM   *Geranium maculatum*

     Wild geraniums are not the kind of flowers that will turn a whole field pink. Rather they sprinkle a bit of color along plain roadsides or in green fields.

FALL ASTERS AND COLORED LEAVES
                                                           Aster genus

Fall winds and rains often make companions of purple asters and the maple's newly fallen leaves.

GREEN FROG *Rana clamitans*

These frogs are most commonly seen sitting patiently in shallow water or on a bank close to the water. One big leap from either position will carry the frogs to safety in deeper water.

WILD GINSENG PLANT   *Panax quinquefolius*

Ginseng is certainly one of the most famous herbs in the world. The ginseng root has been valued as a restorative medicine for thousands of years in the Orient, and many hundreds of pounds of it have been shipped there from the Catskills.

BLOODROOT   *Sanguinaria canadensis*

      Bloodroot got its name from the bright orange-red juice of its thick rootstock. In early spring, from the dead leaf litter in the dry woodlands, the bright white flowers push up.

WOODCHUCK   *Marmota monax*

    The woodchuck is a true hibernator. It sleeps deep underground in its burrow from the end of summer until late winter or very early spring. The rest of the year it is a nuisance for the farmer: It digs holes in the best fields and eats the farmer's garden.

MINK   *Mustela vison*

    The mink is a big, robust, dark brown weasel that spends much of its time in or near water. It is a savage fighter for its size. Like some other members of the weasel family it resorts to a fetid discharge from its anal glands when scared or fighting.

DAY LILIES   *Hemerocallis fulva*

   Day lilies growing wild are usually escapes from someone's garden. Frequently they are found growing along roadsides or in neglected fields, asking only to be allowed to show their beauty.

COYOTE *Canis latrans*

The coyote has always been considered an animal of the western states, but now it has extended its range eastward and can be found anywhere in the northeast. It has been a resident of the Catskills for the past several years.

RING-NECKED PHEASANT *Phasianus colchicus*

This handsome game bird was introduced into the United States from China. It is a bird of the farmlands and other open areas, but it does not winter well in the snow and cold of the Catskill Mountains.

SWIMMING BEAVER *Castor canadensis*

    This very large rodent was reduced to extinction here in the Catskills by the early fur trappers. It has now been returned to many of its former locations and again we see beavers and their ponds along our streams.

GOBBLER BY A STREAM   *Meleagris gallopavo silvestris*

    The wild turkey is truly a bird of beauty, especially in the sunshine when its iridescent feathers flash shades of red, blue, green, and bronze. This big game bird, like many other wild creatures found by the early American settlers, was nearly destroyed by over hunting but now has been restored to many states.

YOUNG GREAT-HORNED OWL
Bubo virginianus

    Great-horned owls are very widespread, ranging over most of the North American continent. When these young owls grow into adults they will become fierce predators, aptly called "the tigers of the night."

INDIAN PIPES
Monotropa uniflora

These white, waxy, pipe-shaped plants are truly astonishing because they contain no chlorophyll. Indian pipes are saprophytes, that is, they obtain their nourishment directly from decaying organic matter in the soil.

EASTERN CHIPMUNK   *Tamias striatus*

    The chipmunk is a little ground squirrel, well known for its food gathering habit. It will gather seeds and stuff them into its cheek pouches until there isn't room for one more. Then it will go straight to its den to unload. Unlike other squirrels in the Catskills, the chipmunk spends the winter sleeping underground.

PUSSY WILLOWS   *Salix discolor*

     Pussy willow buds appear with the first warm days each year, along streams and in other moist places. The furry little kittens are not only a delight to the eye but they are another guarantee that spring will come.

BLUE JAY
Cyanocitta cristata

Blue jays are noisy, aggressive, conspicuous, smart, and teeming with personality. They are easily attracted to home feeding stations during the winter months and it is here that some people develop a dislike for them. The larger, pugnacious jays drive out the smaller birds and gulp down all the bird seed.

PAIR OF YELLOW WARBLERS
Dendroica petechia

This fetching little yellow bird is certainly the most common warbler in the Catskills. It is also the most widespread geographically and the easiest to identify. The pair pictured here are feeding their young in a low-growing hardhack bush.

GREAT-CRESTED FLYCATCHER   *Myiarchus crinitus*

Great-crested flycatchers nest in the cavity of a tree or stump, or occasionally in a bird house. Their nest resembles a heap of trash. They have the curious habit of almost always including a cast-off snake skin in their nesting materials.

HERB ROBERT   *Geranium robertianum*

  Herb Robert has a beauty all of its own with its small pink flowers and fern-like foliage. Most often it grows in rocky woodland terrain, and is easily overlooked.

WOOD FROG   *Rana sylvatica*

These beautiful frogs are found in forested areas, usually some distance from water. The only time they leave the woods is in early spring when they travel to ponds to mate and lay their eggs.

MALLARD DUCKS

Anas platyrhynchos

The mallard duck is the Catskills' best known duck; it is common in ponds and fresh-water marshes throughout the mountains. But it is also the duck most often found in city parks where a body of water is present. Mallards generally feed on the pond's bottom in shallow water.

WITCH HAZEL BLOSSOMS *Hamamelis virginiana*

Witch hazel is a shrub that usually grows in the understory of both dry and moist woods. It blooms in mid-autumn, long after any other shrubs or vines. In fact, most other woody plants have lost their leaves by the time the witch hazel branches become covered with small, light yellow, ribbon-like flowers.

BROWN THRASHER   *Toxostoma rufum*

The brown thrasher is the Catskills' largest mimic and the most colorful one. Its song is strong and clear as it sings from a high perch. This bird is at home in thickets, brushy fields or hedgerows, where it nests on the ground or a few feet above in a shrub or low bush.

FAWN IN THE WOODS   *Odocoileus virginianus*

The young fawns observed alone in their beds have not been abandoned by their mothers; the does are rarely seen, but they are not far away. Their very young babies must be nursed every few hours.

VIRGINIA CREEPER   *Parthenocissus quinquefolia*

    Each fall the Virginia creeper's leaves turn one of the finest scarlets to be found in nature. No matter how many times you have seen this brilliant vine, you always want to stop to admire its unusual beauty.

EASTERN COTTON-TAILED RABBIT
Sylvilagus floridanus

The most common rabbits in the Catskills, the cotton-tails often live in brushy areas and abandoned fields, but they may also be found in your garden. Unlike the snowshoe hare, cotton-tails do not frequent the wooded Catskill mountain tops.

BABY RACCOONS IN THE DEN TREE
Procyon lotor

   Like kittens, little raccoons will nestle close together when they are small. The most common den for raccoons in the Catskills is a hollow tree like this one.

RACCOON FISHING   *Procyon lotor*

    The raccoon searches for much of its food in the shallow waters along streams and ponds. The fingers of its front feet are so dextrous it can locate food by touch alone. As it feels along the bottom of a stream for crayfish or insects, it seldom looks directly at what it is doing.

THE DANDELION'S LAST APPEARANCE   *Taraxacum officinale*

   Occasionally a spring flower forgets its normal season and appears late in the fall, as this dandelion has done. If this small blossom had appeared in spring, it would not have gotten a second glance. But now, among the frosty leaves, its discovery is a special treat.

BIG BUCK IN THE SHADE   *Odocoileus virginianus*

   This velvet-antlered buck rests quietly in the shade of the forest during a hot summer day. Deer tend to do most of
their feeding during the cool of either early morning or late evening.

BOBCAT   *Lynx rufus*

    The elusive bobcat is seldom seen and scarcely ever heard, but it may be living in close proximity to a rural Catskill Mountain home.